34 Days

JOHNEEN GRIFFIN

Archway Publishing books may be ordered through booksellers or by contacting:

Archway Publishing
1663 Liberty Drive
Bloomington, IN 47403
www.archwaypublishing.com
844-669-3957

Because of the dynamic nature of the Internet, any web addresses or links contained in this book may have changed since publication and may no longer be valid. The views expressed in this work are solely those of the author and do not necessarily reflect the views of the publisher, and the publisher hereby disclaims any responsibility for them.

Any people depicted in stock imagery provided by Getty Images are models, and such images are being used for illustrative purposes only.
Certain stock imagery © Getty Images.

ISBN: 978-1-6657-6630-2 (sc)
978-1-6657-6631-9 (e)

Library of Congress Control Number: 2024919808

Print information available on the last page.

Archway Publishing rev. date: 02/10/2025

Dedication

This story is dedicated to the love of my life, my husband bc Collins. He told me this story and helped me write and edit it by reading, listening and commenting on the work.

I also want to thank family and friends who provided feedback and suggestions to me when reading this story.

Prologue

I met bc (Bill Collins) at a party in my apartment complex near the end of my Master's Degree program at The Ohio State University, May 1978. He was relating the tales of his travels in Europe and Africa. I was drawn to his kind face, warm smile and magical aura. Who would guess that we would be married nearly forty years and have two wonderful sons.

The story that follows is one bc told many times. When I retired from Education, we took a three week vacation in Europe in 2009. It was at that time that I began to write down bc's story with him narrating. From bc's point of view, this story is about his adventures, his friendship with Dennis Nash and his sentence to prison in Cadiz, Spain. bc did not want the focus of this story on his use and sale of marijuana and hashish, which resulted in the time he spent in prison with Dennis, rather to enjoy Dennis and his sense of adventure and their friendship. I read much of this memoir to bc and he was satisfied with it. bc had letters, post cards and legal papers relating to his travels, another source of information to make this story come alive. I hope I have been able to convey to you, the reader, the adventures, experiences and resilience of bc and Dennis.

Introduction

The last two months of 1943, 34 days apart, two infants were born. Midwestern Iowa and Ohio families gave life to Dennis and bc. Both second sons raised Catholic in what would become middle class families with four children, three boys and one girl each. They were middle sons between an older and younger brother with their sister the youngest of the siblings.

They met in the late 1950's as freshman students at Bishop Waterson High School in Columbus, Ohio. Their friendship was instantaneous. Both loved music, rock and roll, loved women, loved cars and loved life. They hung out together at Jerry's Drive In, double dated and went to many parties. Girls flirted with them and were in love with each of them. It was a time of peace and prosperity under the Eisenhower administration with a U. S. victory and the end of World War II, the U.S. was firmly in its prime.

bc and Dennis were born just before the baby boom, that generation that came after VJ Day, they who embraced change as change came rapidly. They both identified themselves with the ideals of that generation: peace, love and happiness.

It was during high school that bc and Dennis faced their first crisis in friendship. Dennis was hospitalized with juvenile diabetes, a treatable but life-changing condition. Together they realized the fragility of life as Dennis faced the possibility of a shorter life span and the many complications that can result from diabetes. Dennis learned to manage his condition with diet, exercise and two shots of insulin per day.

College was next for them, then the peaceful time of their youth was replaced by the War in Vietnam and civil unrest. bc joined the Army National Guard to avoid the draft while Dennis was exempt from the draft. There was great unrest in college during that time with anti-war movements. By 1970 students were rioting and protesting on college campuses and Ohio became an epicenter of unrest with Ohio's Governor Rhodes calling the Ohio National Guard to quell the unrest at Kent State University.

Students experimented with drugs: marijuana, LSD, sopers (depressants), black beauty (speed) and other drugs. Women began to have more freedom sexually as a result of the use of birth control pills. In addition, the women's liberation movement began.

Rock and roll music was the sound of the 60's after the folk song era of the late 50's and early 60's. Arlo Guthrie followed his father Woody and Bob Dylan the poet- songwriter was said to be the spokesman for that generation. Elvis Presley who sang the blues in rock and roll helped make the transition into these exciting times. Mass media was beginning to have its influence with the advent of television. Everyone wanted to have a television to watch shows, news and history happen right before their eyes in black and white. This new medium broadcast the reality of violence…. the assassination of President John F. Kennedy, 1963 in Dallas, Texas.

Additionally, John F. Kennedy's brother, Bobby was assassinated while running in the presidential primary that year. Then in 1968, the Democratic National Convention held in Chicago exploded into violence.

Civil unrest had begun with the Civil Rights Movement in the late 50's.

Non-violent sit-ins, freedom riders, the marches on Selma, Alabama, and the Montgomery, Alabama bus boycott. African American men and women as well as civil rights advocates of all colors led by Dr. Martin Luther King Jr. began to have a dream that America could actually become color blind. But with the assassination of Martin Luther King Jr in 1969 major cities in America burst into flames.

CHAPTER ONE

Early life and college

Laying on the filthy concrete floor in a rat hole isolation cell in Cadiz, Spain, Dennis and I had time to reflect, reflect about the journey that had brought us to this time and place. It's a frightening and lonely place to be with only a hole in which to piss, a dirty thin, thread bare blanket over us and rats running over us while we tried to sleep. We were two men, one five feet eleven inches the other over six foot, stuck in an isolation cell that was about eight feet by ten feet or smaller. It was made of concrete, smelled damp and musty and had one barred window very high up, maybe ten feet high. The barred window was our only source of light. Time crept by like a tortoise; seconds seemed like hours. Sleep was impossible on the cold concrete floor that seeped into our bones. Bread and water was served two times per day and the shadows made by the sun and clouds were the only way to mark time. How many days would we be kept in isolation and what would be next we both wondered. I suppressed my fear and tried to be in the now. While wondering what would happen next, I thought about my life and how Dennis and I ended up here.

I lived in Columbus, Ohio raised in the Catholic faith, as a child I believed in and practiced. I was even an altar boy! My given first name was, William, Billy or Bill. My family called me Bill. Quiet and introspective, free thinking, searching, I was tall, with a vee shaped torso and long straight blonde hair.

You cannot believe the freedom I had growing up in Columbus. I picked up my brother Bud's newspaper routes, one in the morning; the Citizen-Journal and one in the afternoon; the Columbus Dispatch. I was able to go pretty much anywhere I wanted. I could buy cigarettes from a vending machine and hop trains whenever I wanted. My family and I lived on Republic Avenue in Linden near a park in a Cape Cod with three bedrooms, two downstairs and one large room upstairs for Bud and me. My dad worked for Penn Central Rail Road, my mom ran a café called the College Canteen.

Back in the 50's when corporal punishment was expected from parents, my brother and I would get beat by my dad with his belt. My mother would say "Wait until your father gets home" for whatever infraction we had committed and my dad would follow through with her threat.

Once I got to high school at Bishop Watterson, I was in over my head academically. I don't know why I had so much trouble and my parents didn't pay attention to my difficulties. In fact, I failed my freshman year. There are two explanations for my failure, one logical and one emotional. When I went to get my driver's license at the Bureau of Motor Vehicle Registration, a worker told me to look through the viewer to identify some letters. I couldn't see anything! While I sat in the back of my classroom and the teacher wrote on the blackboard, I guess I wasn't able to understand that I didn't see the blackboard. The examiner told me I would have a new experience and get glasses. It turned out that I was nearsighted. The emotional reason for restarting my freshman year I didn't know at the time was that I would meet Dennis, my best friend for life.

Around that same year we moved from Republic Avenue to Sandy Lane. By now I had a younger brother Jim and a little sister, Jeanne. My mother included me in the design plans of our new home because she knew I was interested in that. The house design was ahead of its time in 1959; it was a ranch with an open design in the center, kitchen, dining room, living room and two-sided fireplace. The four bedrooms were all around the outside.

I bet you wouldn't think of me as a tap dancer. I was on local Columbus television once a week tap dancing with my partner until my partner got pregnant – and not by me. Believe me I would rather have guitar lessons, but it was our neighbor who paid for my tap-dancing lessons.

Without much ability to sing, I was a member of a singing group called Jason and the Argonauts. The four of us wore matching sweaters like the Letterman. The local girls at the parties and places we entertained screamed at us as if we were the Beatles. Those Waterson girls, so sexy in their uniforms rolled up their skirts just enough to tease. As a young man at the prime of my life, I had no idea how to deal with any of the girls. Of course, I did make out with some of them, and that was the best, played spin the bottle but the furthest I got then was first base.

My passion for art developed in high school although there was only one art class at Watterson. My brother Bud told me about the Art School in Columbus so I compiled some of my work into a portfolio and was accepted into the Art School which later became Columbus College of Art and Design. While I went to college, I worked for the railroad. That was a job I hated! It was extremely repetitive. I was a fireman, a featherbedded job. I rode by the engine and engineer and I basically didn't have anything to do. I was on the train for sixteen hours riding to Pitcairn, Pennsylvania and back. Then I would be "outlawed" and have to stay wherever I was at the time. I would be on the extra board waiting for a call to go back to work. I quit after a year and worked part-time at Swan Cleaners while I went to school part-time.

An abundance of friends surrounded me. I thought it was a because of the magnetic personality and infectious smile of my best friend Dennis. I didn't have much confidence on my own. Dennis the tall handsome model-esque friend I knew since high school. The man who in his teen years whispered his fears about untimely death to me, my best friend. Dennis, the man who carried insulin and needles with him along with the ever-ready Snickers candy bar. Tall, broad shouldered, muscular, high cheekbones and rugged; to look at him one would never suspect he was diabetic.

Dennis almost always had a beautiful woman by his side. He loved the chase... romantic, treating her, surprising his women with special gifts. No, he was determined he would never marry but believed in day-to-day commitment instead. Dennis had also decided never to have children of his own. In addition to the fact that a child he may father could become a diabetic he also had the possibility of carrying the gene for Huntington's Chorea, a horrible degenerative disease. With Huntington's there is a fifty percent possibility of a child to inherit the gene from his parent. Dennis watched his father be ravished by Huntintons Chorea. Like me, Dennis had a sense of adventure and excitement.

While attending Ohio Dominican College, Dennis met many of the friends that became our circle. I found a stately and beautiful old mansion on Broad Street in Columbus that Dennis and I rented as roommates. There Merton Boyd hosted art events for the Columbus scene. It was so exciting when we were there, helping clean the gallery and set up the exhibition for Columbus art enthusiasts. At the time, the Merton Boyd Gallery was one of the top two art galleries in the city. Merton had original art available for sale by various noted artists including but not limited to Picasso, and Matisse.

Our friends moved in and out of the gallery. Howard and Terri lived in the carriage house behind the mansion. Howard, the brilliant valedictorian with hair down to his ass married to Terri, the independent, petite new age thinker who studied elementary education. Donna, worked for Merton and was best friends of Terri and sometime wife to Ralph. Donna later became a chef who studied culinary arts under some of the best chefs in the area. John J the "walking pharmaceutical" had returned from service in the Army and had become a salesman for Amana

Appliances and Molly, a Columbus Public School teacher, dark haired beauty, independent, lover of the arts and friend to all. John Archer was the High School English teacher and later bar tender. Other friends moved in and out of our lives as well.

While living at the gallery, working, and attending Columbus College of Arts and Design I joined the Ohio National Guard to avoid the draft. My cousin Lenny and I drove down to London, Ohio once a month for our weekend National Guard duty. I was opposed to war and the Vietnam War in particular. In fact, I wasn't too excited to be in the military at all.

I put my Anti-Vietnam War emotions into a painting, an acrylic collage I titled *"Kill Not Another's Love"*. I spent hours of time on it with music blasting. When I had the opportunity to enter it in a competition, I did so. Completed in 1969 *"Kill Not Another's Love"* was one of fifty paintings selected to be exhibited in the Ohio State State House. Over five-hundred paintings were entered in this juried exhibition. My painting collage was exhibited there for three weeks.

When I joined the Army National Guard, I went through basic training at Fort Bragg in North Carolina. Although this was something I never wanted to do, I found basic training helped me to accomplish things I would not have done on my own. My weight dropped considerably with the regimen of exercise and running required of me. In addition, I qualified expert on several armaments, an M 1 from World War II, an M 14, an M 16, an M 79 grenade launcher, a colt 45 and a 4.2 mortar.

After basic training and AIT I served at the Guard post in London, Ohio. For three years I performed my guard duties of one weekend per month and two weeks during the summer. Those duties required very little of me until the U.S. commitment in Vietnam increased. It was then that the Army National Guard attempted to get me to "play war". Can you believe the Army wanted me to cut my hair to a regulation cut white walls and all? I felt that order was ridiculous, I was a civilian except for two days a month and two weeks in the summer. When I didn't cut my hair as required; my commanding officer told me I would be counted AWOL at the next monthly guard report and if I continued to leave my hair long, I would be drafted and sent to Germany. Well Germany sounded interesting, as long as it wasn't Nam. I would like to explore other countries; I was single and had no commitments. I was naïve and believed the Army, I didn't cut my hair, was counted AWOL and then waited for my orders that I would go to Germany.

Ok, so the story about being put at the top of the draft list for refusing to cut my hair may seem a bit farfetched. I had been dating a girl named Cheryl, a student at Ohio Dominican. Her father was a big wig in the Army,

Catholic and super strict. Once when I arrived to pick Cheryl up, he asked me when I had last gone to confession! This was none of his business, but by now I was no longer a practicing Catholic.

Anyway, Cheryl became pregnant and said the baby was mine. In retrospect, I wonder if her dad didn't set me up to go to Bamberg to get me away from his daughter. Even though I didn't believe the child Cheryl was carrying was mine, I promised to set up an apartment for Cheryl and me and we would get married. I would send for Cheryl as soon as I could. We wrote each other a number of times. The letters from Cheryl were positive at first until I received a "Dear John" letter from her. Cheryl was going to give the baby up for adoption and wanted nothing to do with me from then on. I guess I was shocked by such a change in Cheryl's attitude but there wasn't much I could do about her decision. In a way I was even kind of relieved.

CHAPTER 2

Bamberg, Germany

I left the U. S. the day after the astronauts walked on the moon, 1969. "One small step for man, one giant step for mankind" Astronaut Neil Armstrong from Ohio had said. This was my giant step. I arrived at the Army base in Bamberg, Germany the day most of the men were out on maneuvers. Bamberg, a beautiful old-world city in Germany was one of the few cities untouched by the bombings during World War II. I fell in love with Bamberg and thus Germany at first sight. I was older than most of the newly drafted privates and hadn't been in military training for a while.

Even though my rank in the Army as an E3 had been taken away and I was "busted" to E1 private, when I arrived in Germany and received my first pay, I was surprised to find that I was paid for the time I had served in the National Guard in the states. This provided me a nice salary to live on the economy in Germany. The Army also counted the time I had served in the National Guard to determine how long I would be deployed so I only had eighteen months left to serve. I rented an apartment off base as soon as I was able, I did not want to live the Army life.

Because of my basic typing skills along with my training in art, I was assigned the job of base army clerk and battalion photographer. In a letter to my family describing my situation and job in January of 1970 in Germany I wrote:

"I'm the new legal clerk, I work for and work with the Adjutant (Lt. Gile), the Executive Officer (Maj. Sexton) and the Battalion Commander (Ltc. Benedict) plus I am the new P.I.O (Personnel Information Officer) which means I'm the battalion photographer. I have over $300 in a camera and attachments belonging to the army that I use. I develop my own film and make my own prints. I also use the camera for my own use."

In a whole new environment, I was assigned the job of guarding the base that first day. I had smoked pot in the states many times, but on this first active-duty day in Germany, I was introduced to hashish. Hashish contains THC that has been concentrated from marijuana plants and it can pack a wollop. I smoked a bowl, then went out to guard the base. I don't remember how I succeeded in guard duty that day, but I did. Focusing on moving from post to post I happily handed over guard duty to the next private.

It was in Germany that one of my friends invented the nick-name I would prefer for the rest of my life, bc. I did not like the name Bill or my full name of William. I did not want to be called Will, Willy or Billy. So from then on I was called bc by my friends.

I continued my penchant for rebellion as I served in the Army in Bamberg. I wanted to have a mustache and sideburns I had worn as a civilian. I fought to have this right and I won!

While serving my time in the Army, I lived in my own apartment and explored parts of Europe near base. As clerk I was able to write my own passes. I travelled to the Holland Pop Festival, an outdoor music concert that followed Woodstock. I saw Munich during Octoberfest went snow skiing and enjoyed flying in silent gliders on weekends. I also loved Amsterdam and experienced much more. I learned about the European out option provided through the Army because, as a clerk, I had access to all Army procedures. Most guys in my unit were in their late teens to early twenties and wanted to go home as soon as their service was completed to what they called the "real world" in the states. Not me, I chose to be processed out of the Army in Europe from Munich and stay for one year with the promise of a one-way (no cost) return to the USA ala the Army.

My first exploration after being out processed was to visit European Art Museums. While on the road, I saw the Prado in Madrid, the Louve in Paris and The National Gallery in London. As an artist, I loved being able to spend lots of time viewing great works of art by artists such as Salvador Dali, Vincent Van Gogh, and Claude Monet. After my time at the galleries, I began traveling up and down the Western coast of Europe. I found the description of travel in *Travels with Charlie* by Steinberg compelling. The quote follows:

"A trip, a safari, an exploration is an entity, different from all other journeys…. A journey
is a person in itself; no two are alike….
We find after years of struggle that we do not take a trip; a trip takes us…. The certain
way to be wrong is to think you control it'"

Perhaps you may think of this time as the dark ages, dark because communcation was limited. I mainly kept in contact with my family and friends through letters. Making long-distance phone calls was difficult and expensive. The only other method of communication was a telegraph which I never used.

I travelled up and down the coast of Western Europe and Morocco over several years after I left the military. I sold leather goods, djalabas, Goulimine beads, and khaftans to head shops and boutiques as I went North in the summer from the coast of Morocco to Portugal and into France or through Spain. I wrote to my family about my international clothing sales where I increased orders from a shop in Lisbon, Portugal from a few baby tunics to an order for thirty-six tunics in three sizes, a profit of one-hundred fifty dollars from one trip! The joy of living and seeing life fresh each day is too beautiful for me to stop travelling, I wrote. A travelling life doesn't become routine, no stagnation of the mind, living in tranquility.

During that first year after visiting the best art museums in Europe, I met Judy. She was a petite energetic, cute girl travelling around Europe too. We hit it right off and began traveling together.

"Hey bc," Judy said one day, "let's go to England together, check out some sights and you can meet my parents."

I was always ready for something new. "That sounds like fun. Let's go there soon," I replied.

We took a boat from France to England. The English Channel seemed so narrow; I couldn't believe it had kept the island from invasion since 1066; especially during World War II and the Nazi bombing. It's only twenty-one miles wide at its narrowest point.

Our first stop after arriving in London was Hyde Park, in the heart of the city. It covers three-hundred fifty-one acres and is the largest park in London. Judy and I were able to set up camp there along with numerous other people living in the park.

We took a tour bus through London visiting many of the top local landmarks then returned to our camp. I don't usually take tours, but Judy and I weren't going to stay in England as long as I usually remain in a location.

"bc are you up to meeting my parents" Judy asked?

"Your parents are here in London now" I said in surprise.

"Yes, they're staying at the Hyde Park Radnor. We can go use their room to have a nice shower, then meet them for brunch"

"Sure, why not. It will be nice to have a good shower and a nice meal."

I couldn't believe Judy's parents were so liberal, open to having we vagabonds enter their expensive hotel use their shower and treat us to brunch. I thoroughly enjoyed meeting them.

Our last sight-seeing in England was Stratford-on-Avon. "Judy, I said, "Shakespeare's globe theater although so old, seems to come alive. I can imagine the actors on stage and their costumes in the sixteenth century."

"I bet you haven't read many of Shakespeare's work, if any of them." Judy prodded

"Well, you're right; the language is so hard to read and understand." I replied

Time to move on to our next adventure and leave England," stated Judy. "I'm ready to go, how about you?"

"I am more than ready."

We went to Southern France upon leaving England at just the right time. Tourism season was about to begin in earnest.

Judy and I found a petite mason in which to live surrounded by banana plants and complete with its own outdoor cat.

I'm not a cat lover. I've never had a cat for a pet, I'm more of a dog lover. My family had a dog named Jiggs, a collie like Lassie when I was growing up. Jiggs would meet me at school and we'd walk home together. But the cat at our small house was cool. He lived outside but stayed nearby most of the time.

"Judy, look at what our cat brought us" I called.

"I don't want to see any dead mice" Judy cried.

Yes, the cat almost always came by to show us his captured, and dead mice.

When my year was almost over Judy and I decided to return to the states together and I suggested she stop in Columbus to meet my friends before going home to California. I brought Judy to Columbus and introduced her to my friends. She immediately became part of the group. Even though she lived in California, Judy would come back to Columbus to visit from time to time and remain part of our group.

CHAPTER 3

Travelling in Western Europe and Morocco

Once I was discharged from the Army, living on the local economy was easy, the dollar was strong then and there was no Euro, no European Union. Each European currency, the mark, pound. lira, and franc paled in comparison to the foreign exchange rate for the mighty dollar. To give my family an idea of the cost of living, I wrote to them when I lived in Spain. To stay in a hotel with a shower cost about forty-five pesetas a day (approximately sixty cents); for breakfast: two eggs, bacon toast and coffee, thirty-five cents.

In 1972, my European out year expired so I flew back to Columbus on the Army's dime. Of course, I reunited with my friends shortly after my arrival. But the Gallery was a thing of the past. The mansion Dennis and I as well as many of our friends had lived in was going to be demolished.

"You've got to be kidding me," I said to Dennis when he told me this news.

"No man, I wish I was." Dennis replied. "The land the Gallery is located on is more valuable than the beautiful mansion in which it was housed with seventeen fireplaces, a carriage house, a turret and an art gallery."

"I guess there's nothing I can do about its impending destruction" I sighed.

"No but some of us plan to remove a few pieces from the mansion as mementos," Dennis told me.

"I decided to sit on the grass across the street from the mansion we all lived in on East Broad to sketch it before it was raised." I told Dennis

"Well make sure you create copies of your sketch for all of us," Dennis suggested.

That's exactly what I did.

Although I was back home in Columbus, I wasn't ready for this return to the states. I wanted to return to my life of travelling, adventure and excitement. After six months back in the U.S.A., I bought a ticket to fly back to Europe. Once on the plane to Amsterdam, I felt free again. Free to live my life the way I wanted, unencumbered by the trappings of modern society in the U.S.A.

In the months and years that followed, I experienced. Traveling light with only a couple pair of jeans, tee shirts and shoes, I met fellow nomads from many different countries. Sometimes I picked them up hitchhiking through Europe, sometimes we met along the road. It was from them I learned of places to see, exotic places and I heard wonderful, interesting stories.

I heard about Ibeza, Tarazu, Goulimine, Fez, and places with exotic names. I dreamed of my freedom to roam and discover; then I worked to make my dreams a reality. I was never interested in geography while I was in school, but my journeys while in the Army gave me a new appreciation of the world and a hunger to learn and experience more. I bought a VW Van for ease of travel, took out the interior seats to make a bed and traveling hotel, then set out on more new adventures. The van had twenty-three windows all round it with extra windows on top and a top that pulled all the way back to reveal the sky.

Just look up a map of Morocco and you'll be able to locate many of the places I travelled. It will help you get more familiar with that part of Africa.

Morocco was one of my favorite countries. There where the donkey had the right of way, time was turned back nine hundred years. The mussein called five times a day for prayer from the minaret, the people knelt on their prayer rugs, bowed facing Mecca and prayed "There is no God but Allah and Mohammed is his prophet."

I rode the Marrakech Express, a passenger train that traveled through parts of Morocco. It was no express, however, people and pets traveled at a slow pace. The train moved so slowly that I sat on the steps exiting the train car watching the red poppy fields go by. Crosby, Stills, Nash, and Young made the train famous in their song from the sixties entitled **Marrakech Express.** I remember some of the lyrics of their song describing the train which had ducks, pigs and chickens, with an animal carpet wall to wall.

While riding the Marrakech Express, the sounds of the train and the view of the countryside triggered a memory of my early trips on a train in the states. As a young man in the late 1950's and early 60's, I rode on the train with my parents from Columbus, Ohio to Miami, Florida. Maybe that was when I caught the "travel bug". I recall riding in the observation car, sleeping in the small berth, and watching the countryside go by. Once in Florida I could have fresh orange juice squeezed from a roadside stand, enjoy the ocean view in Miami, walk along the beach, see the beautiful palm trees and have a break from Ohio winters.

Now I rode the train to discover new cities. One stop I was determined to make was in Marrakech itself which held excitement and mystery.

It had a carnival atmosphere, a deep enchantment of sights, sounds and smells: snake charmers, men walking over burning coals, and women in burkas with only their beautiful eyes shining uncovered.

Another Moroccan city I visited, Fez was the cultural and religious center of Morocco. As a walled city, Fez had stopped marking time long ago. The donkey had the right of way with the donkey's owner shouting for people in the medina to move out of their way. Being in Fez and all of Morocco is a different trip. I can see myself going through many changes. I've become more of an extrovert and it's a joy getting to know different people and experience different cultures.

While visiting and later living in Morocco, I found going back nine hundred years or more in time was just perfect for me. The slow pace was just right, the openness and friendliness of the people lured me to explore more. I was filled with wonder once when traveling in my van in the Moroccan countryside where I had pulled over to sleep. There, in the countryside village children appeared with trays offering me mint tea and bread to welcome me, the visitor, a Muslim custom. I learned other customs when invited into a Moroccan home. The first thing I watched Moroccans do, was to remove their shoes when they entered, so I did the same.

Sometimes, when I was invited to a Moroccan home, I ate with them. They often prepared a traditional dish for a tajine. A tajine is a type of stew with couscous (granular semolina) cooked with spices, vegetables, nuts and raisins; sometimes with lamb. A tajine is also the name of the earthenware pot in which the food is cooked. The pot is shaped so the steam produced during the long cooking process is forced back down from the top onto the food keeping it moist and succulent. Bowls of water were passed around to everyone eating in which to wash your hands. Everyone sat on cushions on the floor around a table. Then the food was eaten with fingers, specifically rolled into thin balls between the thumb and first two fingers of the right hand. Finally, bread was served and used as a food utensil to scoop the tajine and to soak up any drops of sauce left.

Everyone was served mint tea, an integral part of Moroccan life. Mint tea is a mixture of spearmint leaves and green tea. It was fascinating to watch the making and serving of mint tea because it is considered an art form. It is poured in a specific manner and then drunk with friends and family members. Tea drinking is an important daily ritual especially as a drink of hospitality served when there are guests. Unlike the preparation of other food, the tea is a man's affair prepared by the head of the family. It is impolite to refuse a cup of tea.

CHAPTER 4

The Sahara Desert and Canary Islands

One time when I was living in a small house in Tarazou, Morocco I lived on a banana plantation by the sea just North of Agadir. This house was surrounded with trees of fig, olive, eucalyptus, lime and date palms. I took time for yoga, meditation and expressing myself with art in drawings. Health wise, I had never felt better weighing about one-hundred fifty pounds. Spiritually I studied two Eastern Philosophies: Buddhism and Taoism. In the Taoist philosophy, religion and ways of life aim to have humans and animals live in balance with the universe. Taoists believe the body joins the universe after death. Buddhists believe in four noble truths: life is full of suffering, there is a cause of the suffering, it is possible to stop suffering and there is a way to extinguish suffering. I came to believe in Eastern philosophy and religion as my spiritual path and left Catholicism behind.

I wanted to travel to the Canary Islands. There was a two and one-half ton truck loaded with supplies that was going to travel through the Sahara and I was able to hitch a ride with it. I rode on the back of the truck on top of the supplies wearing a Moroccan Burber tuareg scarf that wrapped around my head and neck to keep out the sand. I could picture myself looking like *Laurence of Arabia* in that scarf.

The first stop of the truck was at Agadir, then Iune and Goulimine. There, the oasis at Goulimine. rose out of the desert sand looking like a mirage with its palm trees, cool inviting water, and hot mineral springs. In Goulimine I bought several Goulimine beads from natives. These beads, made from Venetian glass, were beautiful and often used in trading. Next on to Tan-Tan, the second oasis in the Sahara and then Iune. I saw the blue men of the desert riding on their camels and wondered whether they were a mirage or real. Their skin was blue-black from indigo dye they used in making their clothes. The blue men transported goods from Mauritania to Morocco by camel.

With two Canadians and twelve Arabs I continued my journey across the Sahara Desert to Iune. It took us twenty-seven hours to travel two hundred twenty-eight kilometers (about one-hundred forty-two miles), what would normally take a car in the US about five hours. Moving by night, I sat on top of the truck. In the Sahara Desert there are no roads, only sand dunes. A metal track was placed in front of the truck when the wind-swept sands stopped its forward progression. We got stuck at least five times. In a letter home I wrote that the desert is difficult to describe - flat as the eye can see, tan with dunes sometimes as high as thirty feet. The nights are frigid, the sky filled with stars, a sight that is overwhelmingly beautiful. Covered with a djellaba (a woolen full-length cloak or robe with a hood worn over your clothing) I stood the heat of the sun during the day by finding the coolest shade available.

Right before crossing the border from Morocco to Mauritania on the Atlantic Ocean, I hopped on an amphibious craft to a waiting ship where I climbed up a rope ladder to reach the ship. I found out that that ship was going to the Canary Islands and landing at Grand Canary. The ship docked at Las Palmas, a duty-free port. There I saw trees filled with yellow canaries, how astounding!

While I was at Las Palmas, there were ships docked there from all over the world. One of the ships, which looked like a pirate ship, was a one-hundred five-foot Baltic Trader. It was a gorgeous classic wooden cargo sailing vessel. I hopped on a small boat to get to the Baltic Trader then climbed on a rope ladder to get on board. When I met the owners of a Baltic Trader, they invited me to stay on the ship while they tried to amass a crew in order to sail. I hoped to learn about sailing and find a way back to Morocco. I slept below deck for several days and my time there was restful and comfortable. Approximately twenty sailors were needed to man the ship. Unfortunately for me, the owners were unable to procure a crew. However, I met Ed there, an American who had a map with him which showed La Caldiera De Tabriente on La Palma, the second largest volcanic crater in the world. I had a new journey to discover another place.

Ed and I took a boat to La Palma, where I lived near the apex of a mountain top on La Palma carrying food and necessities up the mountain obtained from a nearby village below. I climbed up an aqueduct, then a mule trail, and finally made my own path. The aqueduct was built to deliver water that was mined from the mountains at ten thousand feet up to feed the needs of the villagers below. It was a day long climb up to my perfect cave. I climbed La Caldera as well and walked along the volcanic crater topped with flowers surrounding me; everywhere

I looked - paradise. Here, alone I was one with nature. I watched the constellations move at night in the blackest skies. Here in La Palma, I felt as if I could touch the stars!

I wrote to my brother Bud the following about La Palma. "There the beauty of green in every shade and subtly spaced every color of the spectrum, like the colors used by Seurat. There nature's silence is the ever-constant flow of the crystal clear, cold river, which from up here at four-thousand feet looks like a white ribbon that was tossed by a child in sheer ecstasy. And when you breathe in the morning and night you can feel the crispness of clean fresh air and during the day you can smell beauty. All my senses are awakening."

I am on top of this mountain, four thousand feet, which has a meadow of surrealism, a shallow bowl of figs leading to a garden hiding a cave in an altar guarded by a stone image from another era.

In La Palma, along with watching the stars I was entranced by following the moon's phases. The moon and her phases are my friend, especially the full moon. She blesses my journey; she lights my way. I always prefer to travel when the moon is full. Then I have the right vibes and I'm blessed with good fortune.

Over several years I travelled and experienced many wonderful sights. sounds, and tastes. My lifestyle was an idyllic existence as far as I was concerned. When problems presented themselves, I conquered. I could go or stay as long as I wanted. I enjoyed the isolation and freedom to read/run along the beach/think/watch/look/draw/take care of the basics – I scraped muscles off the rocks in the ocean, cooking and eating what I found. I slept on the beach in a lean to, I lived in a cave. I enjoyed reading during this time and one book captured my beliefs about travel. In Castaneda's "The Teachings of Don Juan; A Yaqui Way of Knowledge", he says "there is only the traveling on the paths that have a heart. There I travel and the only worthwhile challenge for me is to travel its full length."

Just imagine yourself on a beach facing West toward the great expanse of the ocean. It is dusk, the sun hangs on the horizon. If you can wait long enough and watch closely as the sun dips below the ocean you may see the elusive blue flash. It appears for a second just and the sun dips below the horizon.

In a letter to my family, I explained my experiences…." you asked me to tell you about myself. As for myself, it's difficult sometimes relating what goes through my head. I know that traveling is now a part of my life, but returning home is also a part of it." I told them I live in the moment and approach life with excitement and wonder. I am ready to face any situation good or bad. I worked to train myself to feel happy, to do without things.

There were situations I encountered during my travels that threatened my health. Once when crossing from Morocco into Portugal I felt exhausted., When I looked in a mirror, I saw my yellowing eyes. I recognized the signs of hepatitis. I checked myself into a hospital in Portugal where I was housed with other hepatitis patients, many of whom were children. The Portuguese diet of fish and potatoes was a good diet to help combat my illness along with lots of rest. I was in the hospital for almost a month before being seen by a doctor who could speak English. However, not seeing a doctor for a month wasn't critical since it was obvious what had made me ill. Before I left the hospital, I asked if I owed any money for my stay. I was surprised to be told that there was a coup d'état in Portugal at that time, and, therefore I owed nothing.

I travelled to a commune in Ghent, Belgium where I followed a modified ten-day brown rice. This simple diet was designed to cleanse my bloodstream and aide in my recovery. The diet consists mainly of eating brown rice and tamari for ten days.

In another incident, I pierced my hand by a palm frond. I tried to treat the wound myself and remove it but it just got more infected, swollen and red by the day. I was lucky to meet a physician who performed a small surgery to remove the frond and then wrapped my hand in bandages. When I asked him if I owed him any money, he asked me if I was rich. Of course, my answer was "no". So he replied that I owed him nothing.

CHAPTER 5

The Rif Mountains and hashish

After experiencing and enjoying the effect of hashish when I was in the Army, I thought I may be able to find a source to obtain more. Obtaining hash would be another source of income for me and for personal use. While sitting around a campfire one night with Peter and Perry, a couple of hitchhikers I picked up on my way to Tarazou, we talked and smoked hash.

"Hey man." Perry said, "you should come with us on our trip to Katama."

"Yeah, Peter added, "you can learn the process to make hashish, and purchase some from the local Arabs."

"I would love to go with you," I stated "when are you headed there?" "This hash is the bomb."

"We can leave in the morning," Peter said.

"I'm excited to head there with you, let's go in the morning." I replied

I travelled to Morocco and Katama in the Rif Mountains with Peter and Perry. After a bus ride into the mountains we disembarked, walked up a dirt road and into the lands owned by Ali and his family. As we strode up the mountain, in every direction we looked there were marijuana plants, or kif as it is known in that area. What a beautiful sight! Mountain sides terraced with kif. The Rif Mountains, not part of the Atlas Mountains, get the most rain of any area in Morocco. What a perfect environment in weather, temperature and moisture for their main crop.

Growing marijuana, making hashish and hashish oil was the farmer's livelihood in Ketama. Everyone had a role to play in making hash at the farm. The women in their bright multicolored khaftans who carried the cut stalks of marijuana from the fields up the mountain to process; all of their body covered except their eyes. The children who worked in the small processing hut. The men in their earth tone djallabas who grew the marijuana and sold it to customers or used it for themselves. The men smoked black tobacco into which they sprinkled finely chopped marijuana into their pipes called sipsis with a soap stone and long wooden stem. Kif – their name for the marijuana and black tobacco mixture was kept in a leather pouch in a kif bag. Kif, a part of every Moroccan man's daily routine. Although marijuana and its byproducts like hashish were illegal in Morocco, the police ignored the farming, making and selling of it as long they were provided bribes and/or money to turn away.

Peter and Perry introduced Ali to me, a man with whom I would do business over time. Part of Ali's domain sat on a leveled part of the mountain where there were two huts made from mud with thatched roofs. As guests we stayed in a small clean hut on the mountain. Inside was a low round table near the floor with pillows all around. Moroccans seated on the pillows ate couscous from the tajine. We ate with the Moroccan men; the men cooked and served the meal to their customers and us. No women were ever present.

The second smaller hut was where the hashish was made. Inside this hut the walls and ceiling were lined with plastic. As the hash resin drifted around the room, it clung to the walls and/or ceiling. A tightly woven silk cloth, like a cheese cloth, was stretched over a shallow plastic tub as taut as possible. Only the top part of the marijuana plant and buds were used to make hash. This was accomplished by rubbing or pounding the dried marijuana plant top and buds over the silk cloth. The plant resin formed soft green clouds within the hut, floating and landing on the plastic lining inside.

Only the pollen of the plant, heavy with THC, went through the silk. THC is the chemical that causes the "high" in marijuana and its biproducts like hashish and hash oil. After working the budded marijuana against the silk, what plant parts didn't make it through the cloth were pushed aside and new plants were introduced. The best hash was Zero Zero. Other varieties were named: Ketama, Sputnik, and King Hassan. To make one kilo of Zero Zero hashish, it took one hundred kilos (about 220 pounds) of marijuana. One kilo is equal to approximately two pounds. Hashish and hash oil are more concentrated with THC and thus more powerful.

When the tub was full, the fine, soft pollen was made into thin square shapes or other shapes created on a hand cranked metal press heated over a fire. The hash was then compact, ready to be transported, sold or smoked. All parts of the remaining marijuana plant were used, stems, seeds and leaves fed to the family chickens.

While staying at Ali's farm, and watching the process used to make hashish, Peter and Perry gave me important advice.

Perry said, "Don't carry any of the hash you buy out of the mountains yourself."

"Yeah man, one of the family members will deliver it to you at an agreed about location." Peter added Peter continued, "the laws against the buying and selling of hashish in Morocco are harsh. Coming out of Ketama there are three checkpoints: checks of travelers leaving the mountains are random. The police are watching for drugs and drug dealers, so be careful."

Thanks to their advice, I crossed borders successfully many times carrying hash on my person (in my boots or taped on my body) always on a full moon with the right vibes. Hash sale for me was a means to an end. It allowed me to keep on my journey of adventure and discovery. I believed in it; I could always look at the border guards in the eye with confidence as I crossed the border from one country to another. The fact that marijuana in any and all of its forms was legal in some places and illegal in other places made the laws regarding it very arbitrary. It never made sense to me these arbitrary laws that varied so much. I believed marijuana in all its variety of forms should be legal. My belief along with the rebellion I possessed against what I saw as an irrational law was enough for me to buy, transport, sell and use hashish. In my mind I knew this was right to do despite whatever consequences may result.

Once I reached my destination, often Holland, I would send most of the hash I obtained to the states in a variety of containers. I sent it pressed in envelopes, in cans of tea etc. Dennis or Ralph would receive these "gifts" I sent from Europe. Ralph was the wealthy businessman with a taste for the high life of money and drugs. Ralph was a man average in size but big on ideas, never touching it, he bought and sold steel scraps from steel mills, a middleman to other businesses. Ralph and Dennis would in turn use some hash and sell the rest to their friends and contacts. Part of the proceeds from the sale of the hash I received from Dennis and Ralph through American Express. The hashish was popular, a good reliable source, and my friends always wanted and needed more.

In addition to buying, transporting and selling hashish, I continued to purchase clothing to sell as I travelled away from Morocco up the coast to Holland selling the clothing at boutiques and head shops. Sometimes I would pick up a temporary job as well just to make extra cash. I had a goal to set up an import business.

CHAPTER 6

Dennis and the deal

Helene and I met during one of my journeys and started a relationship. Helene was Dutch with dark curly long hair. She fascinated me with her ability to speak seven languages when I could only speak one. After I met Helene we travelled together. Staying with Helene in Barcelona, Spain for a few days I was amazed at Gaudi's organic architecture and almost surrealistic park. We had been following the sun for a while before heading back North.

Helene and I had just returned from Morocco. I was comfortable in my second home of Holland where I lived in Den Hague, The Hague. The apartment we found was perfect for artists as it had great North light. Helene and I were both artists and worked on our artwork. Helene painted, drew and she created incredible embroideries while experimenting with oils.

How I loved the free-thinking Dutch and their attitude. It was my belief system as well. There were cheese shops, a bakery, a clothing store, and prostitutes in the windows of the red-light district. At the head shop, called a café in Holland, I could buy hashish and marijuana. No antiquated anti-drug laws here, no Puritan values. I would listen to the radio to hear the market cost of hashish and marijuana. It was the early 70's, the age of Aquarius, peace, love and happiness. Holland, especially Amsterdam was known for its tolerance and diversity; a cosmopolitan city, it was a perfect place for me.

Dennis suddenly showed up on our apartment's doorstep one day.

"Hey man, what are you doing here" I asked as Dennis appeared in my apartment in Holland? It's great to see you!" When he appeared, Helene was not home so I planned to introduce the two later.

Dennis and I hugged each other as we always did. Without much discussion Dennis blurted out that he wanted us to do the big deal. "I have the means to buy a lot of hash. These small amounts of hash you send home are just not enough, it's time to increase the amount of hash and the money we can make from selling it."

"So, what's the plan," I quipped to Dennis. "I just returned from Morocco and didn't plan to go back there for a while. I have settled in this apartment with Helene and have a good job taking tourist photos at Maduradam. Maduradam is a miniature city in which visitors purchase their photos as a souvenir of their entry.

"I don't have a plan really; I just want you to take me to Morocco where you get that hash you've been sending home. I want to make a lot of it, transport it, then send it home to the U.S. We could both be set for life with a deal like this" Dennis replied.

I never said no to Dennis. I was closer to him than most brothers. I had never done any deal this daring or big and I was apprehensive about it from the beginning. "Ok" I said, "but we have to come up with an airtight plan of where to hide the drugs."

We thought about where to hide the drugs in the VW van Dennis bought once he arrived in Holland.

"How about hiding the hash in the wheel wells? Dennis suggested.

"That is just too obvious, I said. "Perhaps we can try under the roof cover," I thought.

"No," Dennis said after thinking about that for a bit, "we need to come up with something more creative and secretive."

When we bought wooden posts to outfit the van, I came up with the idea to hollow out the posts to place the hash inside. We worked on hollowing out the posts and finishing the inside of the van with a bed while we stayed in Holland. Once that was completed, we would begin our journey to Morocco.

As we worked on the van, I explained my plan to Helene. I have to say she wasn't too happy about me doing this with Dennis, but we were both free to follow our own path. I really didn't want to go along with this plan, but I did anyway.

Dennis and I said goodbye to Helene and let her know we would be in touch if possible. Then Dennis and I climbed into the van and drove out of The Hague. It took a while to traverse the various countries from Holland to France and through Spain.

Once we entered Spain, I planned to take a short detour to show Dennis the Alhambra, a palace in Granada. I took Dennis to the Alhambra because of its beauty and uniqueness.

"Why are we taking this detour", Dennis inquired?

"I want you to experience this beautiful palace. It is one of the most famous monuments of Islamic architecture and one of the best-preserved palaces of the historic Islamic world" I told him.

When we arrived at the palace, we were astounded by the red color of its walls. We would soon learn the name Alhambra came from its ruby red walls. From the outside of the Alhambra, we could see a panoramic view of Grenada.

Though there was a lot to see we focused on the interior and its unique acoustics.

Once inside I asked Dennis to stand on one side of the open area while I stood in the opposite area. While we looked at the astounding Arabic geometric tiles inside, I spoke to Dennis.

"Isn't this fantastic" I said in a whisper.

"Wow" Dennis replied in his regular tone of voice, "I can't believe I can hear you when I am so far from you and you whisper. Yeah, this place is magnificent. Thank you for taking me this direction, it has given me another great experience," Dennis stated.

"Well, I guess we can move on now to our main destination. You may want to learn more about the Alhambra later," I told Dennis.

Dennis and I got back in the van and continued South across the Straits of Gibraltar to Morocco. It connects the Atlantic Ocean to the Mediterranean Sea and separates Spain and Morocco.

"This is exciting and frightening," Dennis exclaimed. "I wonder what this journey will bring."

Once in Morocco, we went into the mountains of Katama, Dennis drove the van while I navigated us to Ali's farm. This time we would have to drive in and out of the mountains, carrying the hashish inside the van. Together Ali, Dennis, and I agreed on the amount of hashish and cost of the deal. We would remain at Ali's the whole time the hashish was being made, sometimes helping with making the hash ourselves. The hash was carefully shaped to fit inside the hollowed out wooden posts. We bought twenty-five kilos of Zero Zero hash (that's more than fifty pounds). This was a deal that would make both of us rich. However, I was happy with my current simple existence and saw no need to change it. But Dennis and those who invested in this big deal dream saw a much rosier future in the life they would have in the U.S. with the money made. Why not, others were successful with this kind of endeavor.

CHAPTER 7

Twentieth Century Tom Sawyer and friend

While passing the time at Ali's farm waiting for our hashish to be made, Dennis and I each shared our stories of adventure. I had told Dennis about my journeys to that point, now I wanted to hear Dennis's.

"Hey man," I said, "tell me about your adventure with Archer."

Dennis began his story: "Archer and I decied to build a raft something like the one in **The Adventures of Huckleberry Finn** and float down the Ohio River." (John Archer was a mutual friend of ours who was an English teacher at the high school level.)

"Our plan was to build the raft in Portsmouth, Ohio and float at least as far as Cairo, Illinois and the Mississippi River," Dennis continued. " The raft was built with empty metal barrels underneath and three-fourth inch thick plywood planks above. On top we made a small cabin four feet high and seven by eight feet square. Our deck had space all around the cabin and was nine by twenty feet altogether.

We treated all the wood with creasote in order to make it water proof. Prior to our trip, we made three sweeps or oars. Two of the oars we put on either side of the hull in oarlocks. One we secured standing upright. The oars were used to maneuver our craft when necessary. Our raft could turn on a dime and move along faster when we both put our backs into getting it up to a respectable speed."

"Wow, it sounds like you made a study raft. How long was your trip," I asked?

"We were on the river for about three months floating and oarring about four hundred miles. We floated very slowly at a rate of about fifty yards an hour hull in oarlocks."

"Tell me more" I said with enthusiasm.

"Archer and I preferred to float at night," Dennis added. "That's the best time to move when the weather's clear and our vision is clear too. It's then that everything is quiet, the air is clean and it's good to breathe. The sounds at night are soothing and exhilirating. The whole experience is sheer delight."

"I love traveling at night too," I said. "It is so quiet at night, when cloudless, the sky is magnificent and the sounds of nature intoxicating. Did you run into barges and tows going down the river? And tell me about how you handled the locks."

"Usually Archer and I could see the tows and barges in time to get out of their way. The big boats would often blow us a passing signal and sheer off a little way from us to give us room. The pilots would often wave at us as they went by. But Cincinnati, Ohio was the worst part of the river for traffic, there the big cruisers and houseboats seemed to disregard us."

"You know locks are built to help in river navigation," Dennis answered my request. "Without the locks parts of the Ohio River would not have been navigable. In Louisville, Kentucky, the Ohio River drops twent-six feet so the locks there allowed commercial navigation. There are nine locks on the Ohio portion of the Ohio river alone. To get through a lock we would pull a signal chain or push a signal button letting the lockmaster know we wanted to lock through. We would have to listen for the whistles and watch for the signal lights indicating if and/or when we could oar through the lock. When the light was green, the lock was ready for us. Next we would pull up and secure our raft taking a line from lock personnel to secure our raft to an outside cleat. Once the lockage is complete, the lockmaster gives two short blasts for riverside and one short blast for landside, then we can exit the lock."

"Neither Archer nor you were that familiar with the possible hazards along the river" I said, "how did you prepare yourselves before or during your journey."

"We had a full set of Ohio River Navigation charts to refer to as we floated along. Sometimes we pulled our craft over to a river town to check the map, to venture into town, to meet friends and make new friends at times. We could just tie our raft to a tree, no one was going to steal our raft."

"Well, D," I expressed my opinion, "you and John had a great adventure together with some possibility of danger not unlike some of my journeys. Now you and I will experience the rest of this adventure and perhaps dangerous trip together."

CHAPTER 8

Leaving the mountains

The hashish had been pressed and secured inside the van's post, it was time to leave Katama. No one stopped us when we left Katama and we began the most dangerous part of our journey. We had to drive the van North out of the mountains with the stash hidden inside the hollowed posts past three random checkpoints. Our plan was to cross the Strait of Gibraltar on a ferry, drive through Spain and ship the VW back to the states from a port in Europe. Remember, I had never driven out of the mountains with hash before. I had always had it delivered to me in Fez. I was pretty nervous about this trip.

We made it through the first two checkpoints in leaving Katama. It was at the third checkpoint that Dennis and I were pulled over, a checkpoint at which I had never been stopped before. We were asked to get out of the van and follow the police. Though the police didn't speak English, we understood what they wanted us to do. We followed the police and went to a room nearby handing our passports over to an officer as requested. The police checked Dennis and me out then walked back to the van with us. It was there one of the policemen noticed Dennis's bag open on the driver's seat. Dennis always had a bag with him in which he carried his needles and insulin. He had been shooting up insulin twice a day since he was sixteen. The police didn't search the van but appeared concerned about Dennis's bag. It was the looks on the policemen's faces and non-verbal communication between them that I noticed. I was sure that the police wondered about the needles in Dennis's bag. I believed the police suspected that we had contraband and of course they did not know Dennis carried the bag to address his diabetes. The police probably inferred there were drugs somewhere hidden on us or in the van itself and that we were drug dealers.

"Bon Voyage" the police said as they returned Dennis and my passport.

"Even though the police didn't do anything to us, I don't have a good feeling about this" I told Dennis as we pulled away from the checkpoint. "Let's hang out in Fez for a while or take another route back through Italy, delay our plans to cross into Spain."

"We have to go now like we planned" Dennis insisted. "Time is going by quickly and I have my plane reservations and tickets to return by around July fourth with a hot woman waiting to greet me."

"Look Dennis, even a hottie at home waiting isn't worth being busted. She can wait a little longer" I asserted.

"You're just paranoid from all the smoking we've done. Let's keep going," Dennis replied.

Against my better judgment and my sick foreboding feeling, we continued our journey. The next checkpoint was at the tip of Morocco at Ceuta, prior to crossing the Strait of Gibraltar and the Mediterranean. At that time, it was owned by Spain and was a duty-free port, but Ceuta is still in Northern Africa. We were pulled over there, an unusual occurrence from my previous experience. Five Spanish police spent about forty-five minutes checking every inch of the van. Dennis was very nervous during this time, pacing back and forth.

When the police let us leave, Dennis told me he had thought about escaping by jumping off the bridge to a stream below. Dennis was an excellent swimmer. He just flowed through the water with ease when swimming. One of his jobs as a teen and adult had been life guarding at a pool in Columbus. Luckily Dennis did not jump and the guards then let us go and stamped our passports out of Morocco.

"Boy, we dodged a bullet back there" Dennis said to me with relief. "We should be able to make it now. I'm so glad they didn't find it. See, you were all worked up for nothing. Everything's gonna be okay, we're almost home free."

"Don't count your chickens yet Dennis, there is still another checkpoint," I reminded him. "Then we'll be in Spain."

I had experienced a few close calls of being caught with marijuana and hashish myself when traveling.. Once crossing with a couple of girls into Switzerland, the border guards were sure the girls carried hash. The girl's van was searched thoroughly and the guards were going to search the girls and me too until one of the girls put up a big stink, yelling and protesting her innocence. She was the one with the hash on her person in her pants. The guards finally let us cross into Switzerland without a physical search.

Another time when leaving Morocco on foot with hash in one of my boots and before crossing the desert, I was asked to take off my boots for the guard to check. I took off one boot as requested. When the guard wanted me to take off the second boot I protested loudly and insistently. I looked straight into the guard's eyes and asserted calmly that I didn't have anything on me; the guard finally let me pass. I knew that I had hidden the hash in the boot that was not searched. When these close calls happened, I was carrying a fraction of the hashish that was hidden in the wooden posts of the van in which I now traveled with Dennis.

CHAPTER 9

Spain and Francisco Franco

While riding with Dennis driving out of Morocco toward Spain, I thought about the current Spanish government and the conditions there. Man, let me tell you, the condition of beautiful Spain and its people was horrible under the brutal rule of the fascist dictator Francisco Franco.

Before World War II, beginning around 1936 the Spaniards fought a bloody civil war in which many countries participated through monitary support, armements and/or mercernaries, a kind of proxy war. The fascists, called The Nationalists, wrested power from Spain's ruler at that time, King Alfonso XIII.

As an artist myself, I recalled that Salvador Dali and Pablo Picasso were two surrealistic artists who created work during the Spanish Civil War. Picasso is the most noted for his work **Guernica.** Guernica is regarded by art critiqua as the most moving and powerful anti-war painting in history. Picasso painted it in response to the bombing of Guernica, a town in northern Spain bombed by Nazi Germany and Fascist Italy whose dictators and government supported Franco.

Another artist who supported Spain's democratic republic during the Spanish Civil War was Ernest Hemingway. Hemingway is known for his depiction of the Spanish Civil War and his anti-war sentiments in general in his novel **For Whom The Bell Tolls.**

Under Franco, the authoritarian dictator of Spain from 1936 to 1975, The Nationalists ruled Spain with an iron fist using forced labor, concentration camps and exécutions to keep control. The regime created a vast secret police network to spy on everyday citizens. As a sign of mourning, the Spanish people wore black during Franco's reign. And I saw armed guards everywhere, even on the beautiful beaches. Now I was riding in a van full of hashish and would soon be entering that country.

When we reached the ferry and crossed the Strait of Gibraltar to Algeciras, Spain, we were pulled over there as we expected, and we waited in hope and fear; hope that we would get past this border and fear that we would not.

The Spanish guards went over every inch of the van even though it had been thoroughly searched before. I suspected that the guards had been informed by someone that we carried contraband. As the guards took the van apart piece by piece each of us thought of any opportunity we may have to escape. I thought I could escape by telling the guards that I was hitchhiking. I had no legal connection to the VW title or license plates, Dennis bought the van, it was in his name and he had been the driver.

We were in a fenced area in a parking lot while the guards continued working on the van. Dennis wandered over to an open gate in the lot. He later told me he thought that the guards would not notice as he just walked away because the guards were preoccupied with the van. However, neither of us would abandon the other in this situation, alone in a foreign land. We were in this together. It was July fourth and our personal freedom and perhaps our lives were at stake.

One thing I had always heard from other people during my travels was to never, never get caught with marijuana or hash in Spain. I was told that the going sentence was six years and a day given by Spanish kangaroo courts. Now we were there in Spain with hashish hidden in our van.

At least two hours had elapsed when one of the guards stuck a corkscrew into the wooden posts inside the VW. Then the guard pulled out the corkscrew and sniffed its tip.

"Hashish! hashish!" he exclaimed. The guard walked over to me sticking the corkscrew near my nose while he repeated "hashish". The guard's hands trembled while he held the corkscrew.

I inhaled the smell from the corkscrew laden with the pungent odor of hashish with pleasure and said to the nervous guard "tranquilo, tranquilo".

The police arrested Dennis and me, we were questioned, our passports taken, my drawing paper and pens and Dennis's bag confiscated. Neither one of us realized at that time that the United States Embassy could not help us. There was no extraterritoriality there, we would be tried, sentenced and treated as any other Spaniard under Spanish law. In the moments and hours that passed, Dennis's and my friendship, loyalty and our love for each other was tried and strengthened.

We were shoved in the back of a police van that was taking us to where we would be held. At that point, neither one of us knew where we were going, what it would be like or how we would survive.

"Man" Dennis said, "this situation is fucked."

"Dennis, we knew we were taking a big chance, now we have to live with the consequences. We are young and strong, and we will be ok" I told Dennis, though I really wasn't so sure myself.

Dennis held my hand and squeezed it so hard I thought it may break. Dennis was terrified! He was used to having a plan and following that plan. To me, after following a journey that led me, I was able to be in the now to take what came no matter what. I had an advantage over Dennis, I had been living in Europe and North Africa simply and at a slow pace for a long time. I had no one to answer to but myself. But I also knew that without insulin, my friend Dennis would die.

When we arrived at the prison, we were pushed together into an isolation cell. Time stood still.

CHAPTER 10

Cadiz, Spain

Suddenly Spanish guards opened the cell door and the light from outside our cell blinded us. "Vaminos, vaminos" they shouted at Dennis and me. We were startled awake in the isolation cell; tired, sore, and apprehensive. The guards pushed us and yelled at us forcing us into the prison's cold shower. The guards indicated we should sit. One of them cut our hair and he pointed to my mustache making gestures of shaving my mustache, I complied. It was disorientating and frightening as we did not know what would happen next. The guards were rough, and we could not speak or understand Spanish.

Although Dennis was provided the insulin he brought with him to Europe, he was running out. Two shots per day used the insulin quickly and Dennis and I were concerned about the conditions under which the insulin had been kept. We devised a plan to stay in touch with each other: I would give Dennis at least one of his daily injections of insulin. But Dennis must obtain more insulin from the United States and quickly.

Dennis and I were given back some of the items we had during our travels. I received my rapidograph pen with nibs and color inks. These I used to create my detailed mandalas.

For the first time since our trip, our capture and our isolation together, we were separated. Dennis was taken to the prison infirmary, and I was put in the main area for prisoners. There was a dormitory type of area for prisoners as well as a row of cells for two. Later I was moved to a cell with one other inmate. That inmate did not speak English, so we had few ways to communicate.

It was a very ancient prison in Cadiz, Spain, Cadiz, the oldest city in Europe. The prison was all stone and concrete, no vegetation was present at all. The only way to see nature was to look at the sky. There was a concrete recreation area where inmates could play handball or walk around.

There was routine, twelve hours in your cell and twelve hours out of your cell. I was assigned work during the day six and one-half hours per day, five and one-half day per week sewing footballs (that's soccer balls in the U. S.). I earn an average of one hundred twenty-four points a week. With points I can purchase items from the prison store which sells basics like stamps, cigarettes and toilet articles. They also sell some extras: milk, ice cream and cookies. We are also allowed to purchase items from the outside such as fruits, veggies, nuts, etc.

There were about twenty different countries represented by the prisoners in Cadiz most of whom were imprisoned for drug violations. There were ten Americans and there were Spaniards in the prison too. We had to figure out how the prison works, how to communicate with our family and friends outside the prison, how to get legal assistance and simply how to live and survive.

At first, I did not want my family to know that I had been traveling with Dennis and was well aware of the risks I was taking. In 1975, I wrote my parents from prison that I did not know the driver, the person with whom I rode. I also told my family that I had no knowledge of the hashish that was hidden in the van. I let them know I would be held until trial but no trial date had been set. When I wrote my family, I had already been in prison for two months and conjectured that the trial would occur within the next two to three months. Boy was I way off with that belief. I asked for money to cover some of the cost of lawyer fees and an open plane ticket. I described the prison to my family writing that my first thought was that a Spanish prison would be one of the worst in which to be incarcerated, but then told them that it is not. The prison is unlike the typical American movie concept of a prison I wrote…. or the reality of prison life in America I continued. No uniforms are worn, no gangs, no fights, no homosexuality. Much of what I wrote was designed to lessen the worry for my parents and family. In reality I felt the imprisonment was very difficult, isolating and monotonous. I had been living a free life of overwhelming beauty close to nature for four years, now I was faced with monotonous routine, monochromatic colors and little contact with nature except the sky.

I wrote "the thing I miss most is nature! There is none here, only concrete and iron bars. The most important point for me," I wrote to my family, is to accept this – I have very easily accepted this imprisonment and more than anything I want you to. I look at this time as a time of progress, a period of introspection and self-karma. For me it is a time for doing yoga, and learning Spanish. As Mahatma Gandhi said "we have a rare opportunity of learning the virtue of patience in prison life."'

About seven hours a day are spent in the courtyard or patio. It is a high walled-in area about ten by forty meters shared with a little over two-hundred prisoners. Since we were most often together in the courtyard, at times Dennis would fake insulin shock and other times he wasn't faking. The diet at the prison and eating only two times per day made it difficult for Dennis to regulate his blood sugar and therefore insulin. Sometimes I would go to the infirmary to give Dennis his shots but most of the time I gave them to him in the courtyard. The Spanish guards didn't interfere with this process as either they didn't understand, or they didn't want to give Dennis his shots.

We spent much of our time outside our cell playing chess, practicing yoga, drawing, learning Spanish, waiting and waiting. On some days Dennis would tell me he was going to fake insulin shock, he would fake many of the symptoms. The symptoms of having too much insulin can include dizziness, sweating, tremors, confusion, headache and heart palpitations. A simple carbohydrate like orange juice can alleviate this problem. Sometimes a glucose solution needs to be given by a doctor intravenously.

The Spaniards had not allowed Dennis's newly prescribed insulin from America into the prison for his treatment, he would have to adjust to theirs. When Dennis would fake an attack, he would be carted outside of the prison to a hospital nearby. At least it was a chance for Dennis to get out for a while, I remained imprisoned. Dennis lived in the prison infirmary most of the time he was incarcerated.

Everyone hung out in the courtyard when not working or cleaning. Dennis and I met Angel, a Puerto Rican by birth, an inmate from California who soon became our main interpreter and friend. Angel worked in the prison office. From time to time, he was able to play rock-n-roll music over the loudspeakers and everyone in the courtyard heard the music.

Eddie and his two Dutch friends, Vincent and Jon were inmates too. They had beds in the dormitory and were often the men selected to mop the dormitory floor. Like most Dutch, Eddie, Vincent and Jon are multilingual and can speak English.

CHAPTER 11

Surviving prison

The prison was cold, not in the sense of the ancient prison's temperature but in the feeling of the concrete walls, floor, and ceiling. Small, it gave a cloister phobic feeling, except for the sun shining on the concrete of the courtyard, cold was one of the constants. Cold water for bathing, cold water to wash your clothes, cold water to move the dirt around on the cold concrete floor with the mop soaked with cold water. Cold showers which did nothing to stop the odors of this old damp, dirty prison.

The smells, the smell of sweat and piss and fear, of men crowded together relieving themselves in the open. Dirty, moth-ridden moldy blankets over a piss and shit and cum stained mattress. Twelve hours in, twelve hours out. Five roll calls per day, three at night. Attempting to sleep under the bright bulb in a cell with a metal door, no bars here. The filthy toilet in the corner of the cell.

The experience of prison is a painful one, always there forever encroaching on your private world an impersonal and indifferent environment in which I am physically contained, a feeling that hits directly at my sensations. Its corridors of refuse, its wasteland approach. So much against my instinct, I want to move and cannot.

I made myself cold. I consciously withdrew myself from everything around me and about my circumstances. I built my own walls to pass through, to exist and survive – to live. In prison, you lose your identity, your freedom to choose when to eat, when to get up, when to do anything without following the prison routine and the guard's orders.

As a prisoner I lost touch with everyone I loved; I had no physical interaction with anyone. Because I continued to have some art materials, I created mandalas which helped me to meditate and focus myself through my mind out of prison. A mandala is a geometric configuration which can be used as a spiritual guidance tool in order to establish a sacred space to aide in meditation. The spiritual journey represented by a mandala starts from the outside of the design to the inner core through layers. According to artist Saudamini Madra," it's all about finding peace in the symmetry of the design and of the universe." I felt, with enough practice and patience I could find peace.

In this foreign country, even though we had each other, the prison was very isolating. Privacy was almost never possible. The bright institutional lights glared constantly. The cold light of a bare light bulb hung above each cell and was always shining. A row of holes in the floor were dug for toilets open for all to see. Dennis and I had no visitors except the American Consulat.

Dennis and I each eventually received orders from the Spanish Court that designated Cadiz as the appropriate prison for our time as inmates.

Dennis and I hired a lawyer, Pedro Fernandez Malero to help us with our case and the Spanish Court. We orally agreed to a fee of one-thousand dollars, five hundred contributed by each of us. We each had to ask for monetary assistance from our parents and friends for the lawyer's fees.

I had a lot of time to think, especially at night. One night I wrote my true thoughts about the drug deal I got involved in with Dennis. Here is what I wrote in a partial letter to Helene :

Let me see – I just told Dennis it seems funny we didn't have time to have a last cup of coffee with you and now we have so much time- time which sometimes seems empty and wasted and for what? What is gained? How does all this flow? Not like the round softness of gently moving water, but more like uncontrollable raging river that suddenly has shoved against a dam. To stop water, lay idle and become stagnant. I'm sitting here with the reality of what's happened within me and I know I'll never again in my life let myself be placed in a situation where any outside influence rules my innermost feelings – for the first time I've not moved with what was in my being but gone contrary to every feeling inside, you and only you know it shouldn't have been. That I didn't want to leave I felt this and told you so and yet I let myself be influenced through friendship or more truly through a lack of belief in myself. If I would have said no to Dennis, it would not have been, now it takes the reality of the situation to understand what I feel deepest inside and for what I believe.

Sometimes Dennis and I could hear the cries of some of the inmates chosen by sadistic guards for beatings at night. Those inmates were then thrown into isolation in the hole. The long nights dragged on and on, with the fear of whether Dennis or I would be one of the inmates to be beaten.

"Oh God," I said to Dennis in the courtyard, "did you hear those screams from the men last night? It was so horrible to hear them, I did not want to imagine how they were being tortured."

"Luckily I didn't hear the torture last night," Dennis replied, "but we should be careful to stay out of the guards way and do the best we can to follow their orders."

I hope we are visited by the American Consul soon, I stated. Then we can find out what our prospects are for getting out of this place.

After a couple of weeks in prison, we met the American Consul. From him, Dan Vernon, we learned we would be tried as any Spaniard would be treated. The United States government couldn't do anything to help us. To receive packages, our family and friends would need to send them to the American Consul. I sent the address to my family: Dan Vernon, American Consul, Seville, Spain, APO 09282 N.Y., New York. The consul would then bring the package to us. We would have monthly visits from Dan. Dennis and I received a few packages and letters from home. We could write letters only once a week and all mail we received or sent was checked.

Dan and later our Spanish lawyer, Malero, told Dennis and me that there was always hope. Hope of a partial or full indalto or amnesty that would occur when Franco died…a tradition in Spain, an indalto upon the death of a ruler. Prisoners in Cadiz believed the indalto would be granted when Juan Carlos became King of Spain retaking the throne that had been his father's. Franco had overthrown Juan Carlos' father in a coup d'etat just prior to World War II. Generalisimo Franco took over Spain in 1939 and ruled forcibly and severely for almost forty years. Now in the mid to late 1970's, Francisco Franco was still the fascist dictator of Spain, but an old feeble man.

Back in the states, in July of 1975 all of our friends and family became aware of our plight. Ralph was one of the first friends to be contacted. He passed the word on to all the rest, Molly, John, Donna, Terry, Howard, Archer, Merton and Russell. Our friends worked to get money together to help Dennis. They were mostly concerned about his survival because of his diabetic condition and their imagined ideas about the Spanish prison system.. They called the money they collected "The Dumb Dennis fund". Everyone contributed as much money as they could. The money was sent to Dennis to use for a lawyer in Spain and to purchase needed supplies.

Spain was mainly Catholic, and both Dennis and I had been raised Catholic, so Dennis' family tried to pressure the Catholic Church to assist us in obtaining our release. They petitioned their local bishop; the cardinal and Dennis' family even wrote the pope. Not one of those tactics worked.

We finally received an order to appear in court. Of course it was all in Spanish. Thanks to Angel, his translation helped us understand what was being said. What follows is a summary translation: "The Provisional Court with the order of the Chamber in a decision of this date issued in roll No 273, in the case number 158/75, followed in the Court of Instruction of Algeciras for the crime of CS. against Dennis Nash and William Collins. The persons who will be mentioned later are hereby summoned, so that on the 20th day of July at the time of 11 o'clock in the morning they appear before the Section of this Provisional Court, located in the Plaza de la Victoria s/n to attend as defendants the act of the oral warning them that if they do not appear, they will be harmed by the prejudice to which there may be a right. From Cadiz, August 19, 1975"

To assist Dennis in particular, because of his health, the American Consulate through Antonio Lorenzo, filed a request with the Court and a response came January 12, 1976. Basically the request said that the best arrangement for Dennis would be a transfer to Madrid where there are better facilities for medical and dental care. Cadiz prison is indicated for temporary detainees who are awaiting trial or are transients. If he agrees, Dennis should write to the consulate and telegraph to try to have him transferred to Madrid. If Dennis is convicted, he will be placed in a more suitable prison that has such facilities. However, our trial was postponed as we waited for medical papers for Dennis attesting to his health and diabetes.

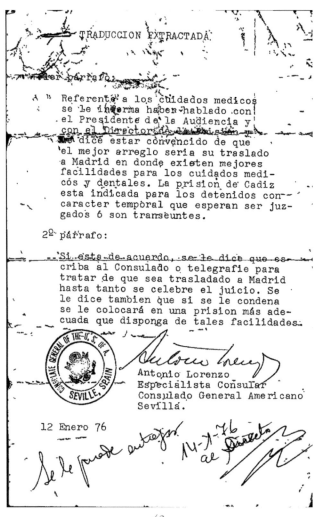

CHAPTER 12

Spanish Court

Dennis and I held on to hope, the one thing we always had to hang onto. Hope that Francisco Franco would die and there would be an indalto or partial amnesty. Hope as we continued to wait for our trial.

Once Dennis was hospitalized for a month and one-half. His health seemed okay but he had trouble with circulation which can happen with diabetes. The Spanish were injecting him with vitamins which he felt did not provide much of a positive effect. Shortly before being sent to the hospital, Dennis asked me to contact our friend Ralph regarding whether Dennis's mother should come to our trial.

"bc" he said, "please write Ralph and tell him to try to discourage my mother from attending our trial." Here are the reasons she should stay home: 1) there is no definite date set, 2) when the convict had only six kelos and under, an additional person has made a difference in the trial's outcome and we had fifty kelos, 3) my medical condition and papers from the doctors may make a difference in our sentence, 4) if a priest speaks for me it may help, 5) if I am given more than a four-year sentence, my mother would be here for five days waiting for word. She would be lucky to see me two times and she would go home empty. The emotions, time and money would be wasted and I do not want my mother to go through this. Please drop this idea Ralph, no matter what anyone else says or thinks."

I complied with Dennis's request and sent the letter to Ralph.

My lawyer, Mr. Molero. filed many questions and appeals to the Courts in Madrid for me. At one point he told me that he believed he could get me released fairly soon. But the judge refused me liberty for some unknown reason according to him. I keep trying to stay in the present and not think of the future, any future. Not to let myself build up false hope, or get psyched up for being released. But with weekly lawyer visits and him constantly telling me I'd soon be free, the reality of all this hits me. I'm now completely aware of the fact I'm here for an indefinite period of time.

I tried to keep in contact with Helene and my family through letters, drawings and paintings. If Helene wanted to visit me, I wrote her that she needed to go to the American Council in Seville and obtain a paper from them that stated that she and I were engaged to be married. I let Helene know that I believe marriage is possible but that it takes four to five months of red tape first in prison. It was then that she wrote me about her doubts about her love for me. After seven months in prison and not knowing when I will be free, all I want; I said in return is for you to get into life and love and be happy

The day of our trial finally arrived after we had been in prison a year. It was not a trial as we in America consider a trial with witnesses, a jury of peers and trial lawyers on each side. In the states we would have most likely been out on bail and if we had to wait a year for a trial, we may have been able to use the right to a speedy trial to dismiss the case. We did have our lawyer to represent us.

The guards forced us into the back of a Spanish police wagon and carted us to the court room. There, three judges awaited us. As we stood in front of the judges the charges against us were read in Spanish. There was no cross examination, no presentation of evidence. We didn't understand much of what occurred because of the language barrier. No interpreter was provided for our benefit. The trial lasted only minutes and Dennis and I were sentenced by the kangaroo court to seven years and a day. Dennis and I were devastated! We just couldn't guess how we would survive another six years and a day in prison.

"bc", Dennis whispered to me as we headed back to prison in the police wagon, "I don't think I will live through seven years in prison here in Spain."

"You can't think of it that way Dennis," I whispered back. "We have to just go one day at a time and hang onto the hope of an indalto once Franco dies, and I hope that will be soon."

Back to Cadiz we returned to the routine of twelve hours in our cells, twelve out, six roll calls by the guards during the day and five at night marking time.

Time, time is the enemy of the prisoner. So much time! While marking time, an unexpected event buoyed Dennis, myself and every prisoner in Cadiz. Dennis's and my Dutch friends had spent their time working on a plan to escape. We would find out about their escape soon enough and how they had accomplished it later.

Suddenly one very early morning guards rushed into the prison yelling at all of us to line up. It was confusing and disorientating to be woken up at two in the morning after the escape of Jon, Eddie and Vincent. When all the prisoners were lined up and forced to answer to a roll call at an unusual time we knew something important had happened but we weren't sure what.

As we looked around the prisoner line up, I asked Dennis "Do you see Eddie, Jon or Vincent?" They were usually pretty close to our location during roll call.

"No, Dennis answered, "I wonder where they are."

We went back to our cells as ordered until it was time to exit for the day as usual. Prison information is one way to find out what was going on and our friend Angel told us that Eddie, Jon and Vincent had escaped.

After their escape the routine at the prison became more tightly controlled, and guards were more strict and angrier. But Dennis, myself and all the other prisoners were jubilant because the three Dutch men had succeeded in escaping. We knew they had been given a twenty year sentence in prison for their crime but now they were free!

CHAPTER 13

Escape from Cadiz

L ater, after being released from prison and visiting Eddie in Amsterdam, I learned the details of the escape. It was amazing that the three men escaped from Cadiz. It was the oldest prison in Spain built in 1792 and they were the only prisoners to ever escape.

Eddie told me about their escape. Eddie, Jon and Vincent had already been in the Cadiz prison for quite some time. Their quarters were in the dormitory, two of them sleeping on bunk beds. They covered the bottom bunk with a blanket that hung from the top to make it darker at night as many of the prisoners did. Their bunk beds were placed in front of a wall of concrete block. This is the story Eddie told me.

"While walking around the courtyard, I discovered a window in the old prison which opened to a cell. Inside that cell, the floor was made of dirt, not concrete. And that cell was adjacent to the concrete block wall to which our beds were located. I talked to Jon about this discovery and we thought there may be a way to enter that cell."

Vincent joined our conversation thinking about how could we get into that space, dig a hole and escape. "Well," Eddie continued, " Since we were often given the job of mopping the floor in the dormitory after all the other men were either sent to work or were in the courtyard, and we were alone, let's see if we can remove a couple of the concrete block next to the bed." We took turns to cut out a few of the concrete block each time one of us had a chance to do so. We knew it was important to replace the block that had been loosened every time one of the men returned to the dormitory.

"Ok" I said to Eddie, "What did you do once you got the opening in the wall large enough to climb through?"

"Once the concrete blocks were loosened and removed, one man climbed inside the cell to the dirt floor. Again taking turns, each of us began to dig under the first wall to reach the outside. The other two of us kept look out for any sign of the guards returning to the area. We even slid the block back into the open space while one of us was digging to hide the work going on." It also helped that Vincent had the blanket hung from the top bunk where he slept over the bottom bunk and the bed was next to the wall. Since Vincent's blanket had been used this way for a long time, the guards did not think anything unusual was going on.

"Weren't you afraid you would be caught?" I asked

"Believe me there were a few close calls and each of us were very nervous during this" Eddie stated.

"There must have been lots of dirt piled up from digging the hole, how did you hide it" I questioned.

"In order to hide the dirt pile, we spread it around the cell floor and then angled it up against the window so that if a guard looked inside, nothing unusual would be seen"

"I think you know we had friends visit us who lived in Holland. As we came closer to finishing this effort we spoke to our friends in Dutch about our plans and our hope they would come help us leave once we exited the prison. Our friends also provided us critical information about the outside of the prison, telling us there was yet another wall to dig under before getting outside. They described where they would wait for us should we be successful in this attempt," Eddie continued.

"We left in the dark of night fleeing for our lives. Our friends met us rushing us out of Spain and back to Holland" Eddie finished the story.

"Escape from Cadiz!" read the Dutch newspaper once Eddie, Jon and Vincent succeeded in their plan. They could never return to Spain; Holland would not extradite them, but they were free!

CHAPTER 14

Release from prison

Dennis and I each hoped and believed we would be released soon because Francisco Franco died on November 20, 1975. However, it would not be until after our trial in July of 1976 that requests to the court could be made. Dennis and I were separated and sent to different prisons after the trial. Dennis went to Madrid as requested and I was sent to Malaga. I mailed my address in Malaga to my family, it was P. P. Apartado #376, Malaga, Espana.

With the assistance of my lawyer, I requested relief from the court. Each request meant more time; the Spanish seemed to love paperwork and everything moved slowly there. The first request to the court was filed July 26, 1976, Mr. Malero asked the court to know the current situation, degree and compliance with release and conditional release is the one that begs the court to grant. The reply stated that the report for conditional release is in the second grade and it fulfills three-fourth parts redeeming the 6-76.

Sr. Director:

WILLIAM ALLEN COLLINS de 32 años de edad,
de estado SOLTERO de profesión ARTIST , recluso en este
Establecimiento de su digna dirección en el Departamento BRIGADA 5
a V. S. respetuosamente,

EXPONE:

Que deseando saber su situación
actual, grado, y fecha de cumplir
con redimir y condicional, es por lo
que....

SUPLICA:

Si a bien lo tiene conceder la dicha
petición

Es gracia que espera alcanzar del recto proceder de V. S. cuya vida
guarde Dios muchos años.

Málaga, 26 de Julio de 1976.

William Allen Collins

Sr. Director de esta Prisión.

Informe Se encuentra en el 2º grado.-Cumple las 3/4 partes redimiendo el 6-X-76

Resolución

Again, in September two requests were filed, one September sixth, 1976. At that point I had completed three-fourths because of my conviction in October I was asking for parole. The response was that my request may be granted if I reach 3rd grade.

Sr. Director:

William Collins de 32 años de edad, de estado soltero de profesión Artista, recluso en este Establecimiento de su digna dirección en el Departamento Bdg Nº 5 a V. S. respetuosamente,

EXPONE: Que estando en 3º Grado y cumpliendo las 3/4 partes de su condena el 6 de Octubre, deseo permiso para propuesta de Libertad Condicional. Es por lo que:

SUPLICA: A V. I. Si A BIEN LO TIENE que le sea concedido dicha permiso.

Es gracia que espera alcanzar del recto proceder de V. S. cuya vida guarde Dios muchos años.

Málaga, 6 de Sept. de 1976.

William Collins

Sr. Director de esta Prisión.

Informe Ver esto bien

Resolución Pendiente aprobación propuesta progresión al 3º grado.—

192143

Another request was sent September thirtieth. Both requests asked for information from the Court regarding my potential conditional release. Once I was at the third grade level in the process for expulsion, I would be closer to my release. The second request concerned my impending expulsion from Spain; the reply said that there was no report for the date of my expulsion.

I found out there is a retired dentist who lives in Spain, Mr. Castelle, who works part-time for the American Consul and helps all the Americans here. He would help me obtain materials I needed later.

Sr. Director:

...........William Collins............... de 32 años de edad, de estado Saltera, de profesión Artista, recluso en este Establecimiento de su digna dirección en el Departamento Bdg Nº 5 a V. S. respetuosamente,

EXPONE:
Que desea saber si esta propuesto para expulsion del territorio nacional y es por lo que

SUPLICA:
a V.I si a bien lo tiene le sea concedido lo que arriba solicita

Es gracia que espera alcanzar del recto proceder de V. S. cuya vida guarde Dios muchos años.

Málaga, 30 de Septiembre de 1976.

William Collins

Sr. Director de esta Prisión.

Informe Hasta la fecha no tiene expulsión.—

Resolución

.192143

In October of 1976, my lawyer submitted a request to find if there was any information in my file regarding repatriation. The response I received was that there is repatriation if there is a letter of repatriation from the consulate of my country.

A letter from the Council of Ministers allowed conditional release in my case. The letter stated: The Court of Instruction of Algeciras and in response to his wishes to repatriate to the United States, in view of the agreement of the corresponding Sentencing Court, the Board of Trustees of Nuestra Senor de la Muced has agreed to authorize his repatriation without prejudice to the resolution that may be adopted in this regard by the General Director of Security and other Authorities involved in its concession.

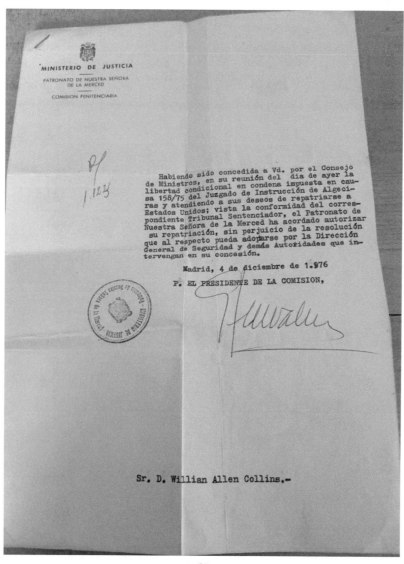

Honestly, I didn't care what the letter actually said; I knew it was only a matter of time, red tape and bureaucracy before Dennis and I were released from prison.

It was a three-step process in order to be released from Malaga and I was in the third step (the Spanish called it third grade). I needed my family's assistance with finances to renew my passport, obtain airline tickets and have some money for travel and I was informed that I should have that ready. I asked them for three hundred fifty dollars to help get these items I need. I asked them to send a money order and not a check because the banks in Spain hold checks too long. I explained that part of the money is for the new passport and the rest for travel. I hoped to repay my parents, friends and family members some day.

My attorney helped me request my passport since the one I had when I was imprisoned expired. My request was granted and Mr. Castal, the U. S. Consulate would bring me my new passport.

Since I knew I was going to have an expulsion from prison and Spain (as it was called in Spain), the time in Malaga seemed longer than in Cadiz. Even though Malaga was better in many ways, there were over four hundred prisoners and it was even more impossible to be alone than it was in Cadiz. The time dragged on, nothing is done on time in Spain, and it is always manana.

I missed letters when I was in transit from Cadiz to Malaga. Then it took time to adjust to the new environment. In August 1976, I told my parents not to send any money to my lawyer, Mr. Malero unless I write to them to request additional funds. The original agreement for his services was five hundred dollars each which was paid because of my parents help. Then Mr. Malero said he wanted one thousand dollars from me if he could get my immediate release – that never happened. All the work to get us a shorter sentence was accomplished by Dennis, our friends in the states and his parents.

At first, I was told my release date would be the sixth of October. I was finally released in December on Christmas Day, December of 1976 from Malaga, Spain. Dennis had been released earlier from Madrid and immediately flew back to the United States.

In December of 1976 I wrote to my parents the following:

> "I expected to be out long before this. I have been "free" for sixteen days now. Usually, the wait for orders from Madrid is eleven to twelve days. The consul came and left my money, passport and plane ticket here with the administration and told me Madrid signed my expulsion order, now nine days ago. Perhaps I'll leave today or tomorrow. The consul comes again soon so I'll check with them. I'll write again when I'm free. Wishing all of you a happy and peaceful Christmas and New Year. See you soon. Thank you for everything and all my love to all of you! Love Bill"

Once released I sent a quick note to my parents to tell them I was free and that I planned to live in Holland.

I left prison in Malaga and despite advice to go anywhere but Morocco, I went to Morocco anyway. I was escorted from Malaga to an airport by the police, and I hopped on a plane to Rabat, Morocco. I was headed to Katama, I wanted to see Ali again. I wanted to talk to Ali about what had happened. I suspected that Ali had told the police about the hashish deal. But when I arrived at the marijuana farm, Ali was gone.

I left Morocco then and travelled to Europe where I stayed for another six months. When I left prison, I was told that I could not cross into Spain after serving my sentence, but when I tested that information, I found out otherwise. I had paid my dues with a prison sentence in Spain and could cross its border.

When I returned to Holland, I looked for Helene, she was living with Zeto at this time. I settled in Holland and with the help of Helene I got a job working for the "House of Yellow" roadies who set up concerts for all performers coming to the Netherlands. There I was given the opportunity to work at Eric Clapton's ***"461 Ocean Boulevard"*** tour. What an exciting and fun job, I looked forward to working with The House of Yellow in the future.

I sent my address and a post card to my family so we could be in touch. I received a letter from my sister Jeanne in April 1977. She wrote me that the family would be celebrating my parents fortieth wedding anniversary in June and that I should fly home. She sent me an open one-way plane ticket with the letter. Jeanne said my mother was ill and I may not see my mother again if I didn't come home. Even though I didn't want to leave Holland, I decided to fly home arriving just in time for my parents anniversary party in June.

Epilogue

bc and Dennis both returned to live in Columbus for the remainder of their lives. They were always the best of friends. Dennis became an appraiser for Nash Realtors, while bc started his sole ownership sign business.

Dennis never married while bc married at the age of thirty-six after meeting Johneen Griffin. Together, bc and Johneen became urban pioneers in Columbus's Short North, rehabbing an old home built in 1898. Two sons, Keith and Kyle were born while they lived on Hamlet Street in Italian Village.

When Dennis moved to Boise, Idaho for a few years, bc and Johneen travelled to visit Dennis and see the country in a VW Westfalia camper with Keith, age eleven and Kyle age nine. Dennis returned to Columbus a few years later.

bc lost Dennis to a sudden death in 2004, a heart attack felled his great friend shortly after his sixtieth birthday. At the end of 2020, sixteen years later, bc left this earth on a full moon. The world lost two great men.

Here is a website with more information about bc's sign making and some of his art. http://www.worthingtonmemory.org/explore/people/collins-william-bc-bill.

The Open Road

Answer the call

Of the open road

Its siren song

Lasts on and on

Many the ways

To travel around

Trips and journeys

Men have found

Gather friends along

Your path, some come

Some go, some

Lovers you know.

Answer the call

Of the open air

Its fresh free breeze

Blows through your hair

No doors or windows

To close you in

Unknown vistas

Whisper begin

Always starting

Never end

You've gone ahead on a journey

I'll catch up one day my friend

.5-23-04 by Johneen Griffin

About The Author

Born in Chicago, Illinois, Johneen grew up in the suburbs. Columbus, Ohio became her home in the 1970's where she met William, bc, Collins her husband of nearly 40 years. She is a retired Special Education teacher and administrator and a mother of two sons; grandmother of two granddaughters Johneen enjoys writing poetry. This story, 34 Days, is her first attempt at writing and publishing prose.

Printed in the United States
by Baker & Taylor Publisher Services